GW00385645

ACKNOWLEDGEMENTS

Thanks to Colm Bryce, Sally Campbell, Joseph Choonara, Donny Gluckstein and Celia Hutchison whose advice and expertise made it possible to write this book and to many more people for their insights and discussions. Thanks also to Chris Ayton at Bookmarks and staff at the Working Class Movement Library in Manchester for their help with finding sources and to Simon Guy and everyone else who has helped with the production of the book.

ABOUT THE AUTHOR

Camilla Royle has a PhD in geography from King's College London. She is a member of the International Socialism editorial board and is a member of the Socialist Workers Party.

COVER IMAGE: A young Friedrich Engels
INSIDE FRONT: A sketch of unemployed workers in Manchester during the Cotton Famine of 1962
INSIDE BACK: Engels (third from left) in Zurich in 1883 with fellow Marxists Clara Zetkin (second from left) and August Bebel, both leading members of the Social Democratic Party of Germany

Published by Bookmarks Publications 2020
Copyright Bookmarks, 1 Bloomsbury Street, London WC1B 3QE
ISBN print edition: 978-1-912926-54-1
ISBN Kindle: 978-1-912926-55-8
ISBN ePub: 978-1-912926-56-5
ISBN PDF: 978-1-912926-57-2
Series design by Noel Douglas
Typeset by Bookmarks Publications
Printed by Halstan & Co

A Rebel's Guide to
ENGELS

CAMILLA ROYLE

★ 1:
AN UNLIKELY
REVOLUTIONARY

Friedrich Engels was born on 28 November 1820 in Barmen (now Wuppertal) in what is now Germany. Despite being from a fairly wealthy family he went on to become one of history's most important revolutionary socialists. He was a disappointment to his parents and a traitor to his class.

His father had inherited a successful cotton thread bleaching and spinning works and set up a partnership with the Ermen brothers, Godfrey and Peter. The young Friedrich, the oldest of eight children, enjoyed a comfortable, middle-class and staunchly Protestant upbringing.

At this time, Europe looked very different from today. After the French Revolution of 1789, Napoleon Bonaparte's forces had swept across the continent. But by the time of Engels' birth, Napoleon had been driven into exile and the monarchy restored in France. The forces of reaction were reasserting themselves. Germany would not be unified until 1871. In 1820 it was a collection of 39 statelets, often grand duchies and principalities, dominated by a large and powerful kingdom, Prussia, in the north and by the Austrian Empire in the south.

There was very little political freedom as the various monarchs were anxious to suppress radical ideas — especially foreign ideas. With restrictions on freedom of speech, culture played an important role in political life. Engels played a role in this cultural ferment. As a teenager he hoped to be a writer and penned a play called A

Pirate Tale, a thinly veiled call for revolt against tyranny and injustice, as well as poems and drawings.

Engels' personality comes across in some of his letters, for example when he teases his friend Fritz Graeber for being slow to write back to him: "You fellows always let yourselves be put off writing by 'this and that'. Tell me, can't you write to me for half an hour each day after you get a letter from me? Then you'd be finished in three days." (20 January, 1839)

The Rhineland district where Engels lived was a centre of the textile industry and he was schooled in the realities of industrial capitalism from a young age. In a series of letters to the liberal *Telegraph für Deutschland* written in 1839 (when he was still just 18), Engels described the situation in Barmen and nearby Elberfeld. He showed how factory work was leading to widespread illness and misery: "Work in low rooms where people breathe more coal fumes and dust than oxygen... is bound to deprive them of all strength and joy in life." The sluggish waters of the river Wupper ran red, not with blood but with pollution from the surrounding dye works. In these letters Engels railed against the hypocrisy of the religious factory owners. These treated their workers worst of all, driving them into poverty under the pretext of trying to stop them from getting drunk.

The young Engels was already a brilliant journalist. The letters, written under the pseudonym "Oswald", caused a sensation and the edition of the journal sold out. People wondered who could have written them and Engels was quick to out himself as the author to his friends: "The author is the writer of these lines, but I advise you not to say anything about it, I could get into a hell of a lot of trouble" (quoted in Tristram Hunt, *The Frock-Coated Communist*, Penguin, 2010, p40).

Engels started working for the family textile business at the age of 16. At 18, his father, already worried that his son was becoming a radical, sent him off to work in Bremen as a clerk. But this merely put him into contact with others with similar views. Like many intellectuals of his generation, Engels was attracted to the idea of uniting German-speaking people in a single state and looked to the 1789 revolution in France for inspiration. At this point he held ideas that would now be seen as more liberal than socialist; he favoured free trade and saw the key questions as freedom of the press and representative government. But at the time even liberal nationalist ideas, atheism and opposition to monarchy, would have been viewed as close to terrorism.

In 1841-2 Engels carried out his military service in Berlin. While there he was able to attend lectures at the university even though he was not registered as a student. He took the opportunity to go to parties, drink, smoke cigars, and take up fencing. He started to cultivate his famous facial hair and even held a "moustache evening" where he gathered together his "moustache-capable" friends and put the argument that they should all start wearing moustaches.

In Berlin he developed an interest in philosophy and came across the Young Hegelians. This group of philosophers were influenced by the great German philosopher GWF Hegel (1770-1831). Hegel was the first to show how the whole world is in a constant process of change and transformation.

In the 1840s, even though Hegel had been dead for

ten years, there was an ongoing battle over his legacy that was not helped by ambiguities in his own work. Hegel had at one point been a supporter of the French Revolution, but in his later years he had come to support the Prussian state and to see this state as the end point of historical progress. Some of his followers pursued this more conservative interpretation and were known as the "right Hegelians". By contrast, the Young Hegelians or left Hegelians were drawn to his ideas because they stressed change and development, the development of human freedom under the power of rational ideas. They wanted to hold everything up to the light of reason. One influential philosopher associated with them was Ludwig Feuerbach. In his book *The Essence of Christianity* he argued that the Christian god was a reflection of human desires and would not exist without humanity.

This debate was about more than philosophy. The German speaking states were not as industrialised as Britain and did not have the same combative working class movements. This meant that the key discussions of the day were taking place in the realm of philosophy. As Karl Marx would later say: "the Germans thought what other nations did."

Like some of the other Young Hegelians, particularly Feuerbach, Engels' ideas started to change and he became more interested in the situation of the poor and in the common ownership of property. In Cologne he met Moses Hess, one of the first German philosophers to turn to communism and a founder of the radical *Rheinische Zeitung* newspaper. Hess' communism, and his prediction that there would soon be a revolution in England, were a key influence on Engels.

With restrictions on freedom of the press slightly relaxed, Engels started to write for the *Rheinische Zeitung*. In late 1842 the paper was edited by Marx, who had by this time completed his doctorate but had turned to political journalism after his radical views made it difficult to get academic work. Marx was starting to break with the Young Hegelians by this point as he had started to believe that social revolution, rather than the power of ideas, would bring about change. He was already widely admired and was even described by Hess as "the greatest living philosopher." However, despite being two years younger, Engels was actually much more widely published, with 50 published articles and pamphlets.

Marx and Engels would later become close friends and collaborators. But when they first met, in 1842, Marx did not think much of Engels, who he regarded as still too close in his politics to the Young Hegelians.

★ 2:
THE
WORKING CLASS
IN ENGLAND

In November 1842 Engels moved to Manchester to work for the English branch of Ermen and Engels. Soon after arriving, he met an Irish woman called Mary Burns with whom he would have a personal relationship for the rest of her life. It is possible that Mary worked in the Engels and Ermen factory, although some historians suggest that she sold oranges from a stall. The couple were from very different worlds; Engels was well-read and from a privileged background, whereas Mary and her sister Lydia ("Lizzie") were working class, uneducated and daughters of a mill worker.

However, it seems that Mary educated Engels as much as the other way around. She showed the young German the way that ordinary people lived, acting as his guide to the warren of narrow streets and alleyways of the city.

At this time Chartism was attracting high levels of support among working class people, especially in the north of England. The Chartists demanded universal male suffrage, payment for members of parliament (so that people who weren't privately wealthy could become MPs) and annual general elections. For its working class supporters, suffrage was seen as a means to win better working conditions

In May the Chartists had presented a petition to parliament with an estimated 3.3 million signatures but it was rejected. By August a general strike had broken out after wages in Stalybridge and Ashton had been cut by 50 percent. The strikes were known as the Plug Plot Riots as workers went from mill to mill pulling boiler plugs out of the steam-powered machinery to stop production. The movement grew to involve half a million workers and on 9 August 1842 thousands marched into Manchester and went around encouraging other workers to join the strikes. The Charter was one of their demands.

The National Charter Association was highly organised, with different branches according to different types of industry and collections of weekly subs. Engels became a supporter of the Chartists and a regular reader of their paper, *The Northern Star*. He befriended the weaver and Chartist leader James Leach, whose first-hand account of conditions for workers would be influential on his own research. Visiting the Hall of Science, a 3,000 capacity venue that was often packed on a Sunday, he described how workers spoke there with passion and clarity.

Inspired by these events, Engels started working on his first book, *The Condition of the Working Class in England*. Engels dedicated his book to the British working class, describing how he had forsaken the "champagne of the middle classes" in order to spend time with working people learning about their grievances and their struggles.

The book was aimed at a German audience rather than a British one. Engels wanted to show German readers how the working class lived. Although the effects of the Industrial Revolution were most acute in England, industry would soon arrive in Germany too. But he was also engaging in a theoretical debate among German intellectuals. By this time, he was moving away from his earlier Hegelianism which stressed the role of ideas and starting to develop a more concrete analysis of capitalism. He recognised that the system divides people into a bourgeois class who own the means of production and a working class who own nothing but their ability to labour. Engels started to place much more emphasis on the ways in which economic relations shape society and formed the basis of the clash between different classes.

In the introduction to *The Condition of the Working Class in England*, Engels states that the history of the English working class started with the invention of the steam engine. By the 1820s, power looms were adopted on a large scale in the weaving industry. The introduction of these machines meant that commodities could be produced in much greater amounts and more cheaply. For example, it was no longer economical to produce woven goods using a spinning wheel and a handloom.

The new technologies meant that people went from living in the countryside and working at home with their families, to seeking work in the cities. Engels estimates that the population of Lancashire, the centre of the cotton industry, increased ten-fold in 80 years. Cotton imports grew from about five million pounds of raw cotton in 1775 to 600 million in 1844. The growth of industry also had an international impact as cotton was grown by slaves in North America and manufactured goods were exported. Vast wealth was channelled into the hands of a minority.

Engels' book is grim reading. He describes people working from early in the morning until late at night in the factories and mills. They start work at a young age and work themselves into an early grave doing hard, boring, repetitive work that leaves them sick and disabled. Engels quotes from physicians who described how workers' spines and legs became deformed due to long hours of standing up. Their wages are low and the bosses will pay them in rotten food instead of cash if they can get away with it. The exhausted workers go home to damp and crowded accommodation. There is often not enough food; while the better paid workers can afford meat, the poorest live on only "bread, cheese, porridge and potatoes" and, if there is no work, some starve to death. Many have hardly enough clothing and their homes are "badly ventilated, damp and unwholesome."

Engels describes one of the poorest areas of London, St Giles, in this way: "The filth and tottering ruin surpass all description. Scarcely a whole window-pane can be found... Heaps of garbage and ashes lie in all directions, and the foul liquids emptied before the doors gather in stinking pools" (*The Condition of the Working Class in England*, Penguin Classics, p71). Memorably, he recalls the case of Ann Galway who was found dead at the age of 45 in a room she shared with her husband and son. The room had no furniture whatsoever, only piles of feathers as bedding, and a corner of the floor had been torn up to use as a toilet. Her body was nearly naked, starved and bitten by vermin (p73). Engels accused the bourgeoisie of "social murder"; they had knowingly put people into a situation where early death was inevitable.

According to Engels, one effect of the influence of the factory system was the "dissolution of the family", just one way in which it was transforming social relations. Families had previously worked together in order to produce goods. For example, families worked as a unit in the cotton spinning industry. But with industrial capitalism this was beginning to be undermined. Children went out to work and gave a portion of their wages to their parents, treating the family home more like a boarding house.

The book is not beyond criticism. Engels uses language to refer to Irish migrants that socialists would not use today. He says, "they have grown up almost without civilisation" and have brought "filth and drunkenness" with them (pp123-126). He also makes very moralistic statements about young women and uncritically repeats some of the indignant reports of teenage drinking and gambling of his liberal sources: "In an ale-house which the commissioner visited, there sat forty to fifty young people of both sexes... Here and there cards were played, at other places dancing was going on, and everywhere drinking" (p216). These attitudes are of course all the more surprising given that Engels also enjoyed drinking and parties.

But despite these flaws, *The Condition of the Working Class in England* is an impressive example of socialist history. It combines observations of the way things are with analysis of why they are that way and outrage that they are not different. Marx would revisit this work years later and refer to in his masterpiece, *Capital*.

As well as acquainting the proletariat with crushing poverty, life in cities brought them into contact with radical ideas. Engels argued that workers joined the labour movement "just in proportion as their handicraft has been invaded by the progress of machinery" (p65). Engels had seen the potential for mass struggles among the militant Chartists. With hindsight, his prediction of certain victory for the British proletariat looks over-optimistic. Perhaps though, given the times of mass struggle he lived through, it is understandable that the young Engels would look forward to a coming revolution.

★ 3:
HISTORICAL MATERIALISM

In 1843 Marx, now married to Jenny von Westphalen, moved to Paris as censorship made it impossible to carry out journalistic work in Germany. Engels visited Paris the following year and met Marx once again. Despite their initial frosty introduction, Marx and Engels now started to work together, forming an intellectual and political partnership that would lay the foundations of Marxist thought today. Marx and Engels had more or less independently reached the same conclusions about the importance of the working class; Engels by observing workers in England and Marx through his reporting of the revolts of the Silesian weavers, where thousands of workers took strike action and smashed machinery in protest at declining wages and living standards.

While in Manchester, Engels had produced a significant article on economics, "Outlines of a Critique of Political Economy" for the journal that Marx now co-edited, the *Deutsch-Französische Jahrbücher*. It showed that Engels was not just capable of observing the way in which the working class lived but could combine this with an acute economic analysis. The article, as well as denouncing the immorality and hypocrisy of the capitalist class, contains numerous insights about the inner workings of the economic system and prefigures some of the arguments Marx would later make in *Capital*. For example, Engels starts to refer to labour as the source of wealth under capitalism.

Engels also strongly attacks the "vile" theories of

Thomas Malthus, who had argued that overpopulation was to blame for scarcity and opposed measures to help the poorest. According to Engels, it is only under conditions of competition, where humans are valued according to the wages they are paid and periodic crises throw many of them out of work, that a surplus population can appear to be a problem for society.

Marx and Engels worked on a critique of Bruno Bauer, called *The Holy Family: A Critique of Critical Criticism.* Bauer was a former Young Hegelian who had come to adopt an elitist attitude, dismissing the masses as the enemies of "reason." Marx and Engels initially worked together on this pamphlet, but when Engels left in September 1844 to go back to Barmen, he — perhaps foolishly — left Marx to finish the manuscript and found that Marx had added considerably to the length.

Back in his parents' house, Engels worked on his manuscript of *The Condition of the Working Class in England* for publication. But Barmen had not escaped class politics. Engels and Hess gave a communist meeting there in 1845 that attracted 200 people. All of this horrified Engels' respectable father and his relationship with his parents became increasingly difficult. It also brought Engels to the attention of the police and the mayor, who banned any further communist meetings.

Meanwhile, Marx was expelled from Paris and moved again, this time to Brussels where Engels joined him. They spent many long evenings together working on a manuscript that would later be referred to as *The German Ideology*, with Engels writing most of the text.

In *The German Ideology*, Marx and Engels demonstrated several of their key ideas. Their shared insight was that to understand history, the most important place to start was with the real lives of actually existing human beings and their activities, rather than the thoughts in their heads, as idealist thinkers do. They recognised that humans are part of the natural world, stating that: "The first premise of all human history is, of course, the existence of living human individuals." Some kind of relationship with the rest of nature is common to humans and other animals. But Marx and Engels also argued that humans began to distinguish themselves from other animals in that they produce changes in their environment in a conscious and directed way.

Furthermore, both had come to acknowledge the role of economic relations between people in shaping their lives. Throughout history, humans have lived in very different forms of society, including hunter-gather societies, ancient slave societies, feudalism and industrial capitalism. For Marx and Engels, these different ways of organising society in order to produce the means of existence also produced different social relations between people. The relationship between a worker and an industrial capitalist was very different than that between a serf and a feudal lord.

Marx and Engels distinguished between what they called the forces of production and social relations. Forces of production are the means humans have available to them in order to produce things. They can include human labour, materials, knowledge and technology. These forces, as they develop, can sometimes come into conflict with the existing social relations, creating the basis for revolutionary change and the replacement of old social relations with new ones.

As Marx and Engels pointed out, capitalism ripped

apart the feudal system, in the process creating a growing working class. As the system is dependent on their labour power, workers have both the interest and the ability to cause its downfall. Capitalism created a situation where workers were concentrated together, often in large workplaces, producing commodities for a boss to sell. This situation makes it possible for workers to organise together in large numbers for the first time. But it is not inevitable that workers recognise their power and lead a socialist revolution. The contradictions within the capitalist system could also lead it down a route towards barbarism. But the potential exists for a better society to come about.

Marx and Engels also argued that in any society the ruling ideas are the ideas of the ruling class. Under capitalism, the capitalist class are able to make it seem like their society is natural. It was quite widely believed in Victorian England that the rich get to their position at the top of society through their own merit and hard work. So, the way in which society is organised exerts an influence on the cultural norms and ideas that come to dominate.

David McLellan argues that *The German Ideology* is "probably the most extended description of their materialist conception of history" that Marx and Engels ever wrote (McLellan, *Engels*, Fontana Modern Masters, 1977, p17). Although it was not completed or published in their own lifetime, it nevertheless helps to shine a light on their approach to philosophy at this time.

★ 4: SLEEPING ON A VOLCANO

For Marx and Engels, it was vital that communists group together in an organisation. Engels was particularly interested in building links between revolutionaries across the continent. But this was not always easy. In 1846 Engels moved to Paris where he took part in meetings of the League of the Just, made up largely of socialists from artisan backgrounds. The most prominent influence on the League was Wilhelm Weitling, a tailor and inventor who demanded an immediate socialist uprising. Weitling's ideas were gaining popularity and seemed very radical. But he assumed that revolution could be won by a small minority on behalf of the masses. Also influential were the so-called "true socialists" who emphasised the moral education of the mass of people. Both these ideologies downplayed the class conflict that Marx and Engels had come to see as necessary for communist revolution.

Engels had more success in the League's London branch the following year. He was able to transform the organisation from a secret society to an agitational organisation. The name was changed to the Communist League and the slogan from "all men are brothers" to "Working men of all countries, unite!" Marx and Engels were tasked with producing a statement of the new organisation's politics, a document which would become *The Communist Manifesto*.

The *Manifesto* has since become one of the best-known explanations of revolutionary thought. As Chris

Harman has argued: "It is still able to explain, as mainstream economists and sociologists cannot, today's world of recurrent wars and repeated economic crisis, of hunger for hundreds of millions on the one hand and 'overproduction' on the other" (Harman, Introduction to *The Communist Manifesto*, Bookmarks, 2010, p3).

It was Engels who wrote the first draft, *Principles of Communism*, in the form of 25 questions and answers. Although it doesn't contain all the rhetorical flourishes of the *Manifesto*, it demonstrates Engels' particular ability to write in a succinct and accessible style.

Engels explains how capitalism developed and created a working class and also how the system periodically goes into crisis. According to Engels, the forces of production in capitalism had grown to such an extent that capitalist social relations had become a fetter on these forces: "These mighty and easily extended forces of production have so far outgrown private property and the bourgeoisie, that they threaten at any moment to unleash the most violent disturbances of the social order. Now, under these conditions, the abolition of private property has become not only possible but absolutely necessary."

Engels also describes the kind of measures a revolutionary government might initially put in place, including nationalisation of the land, factories and banks, "great palaces as communal dwellings" and free education for all children. But these measures were intended by Engels to be transitional. Communism would eventually transform people's lives in more fundamental ways leading to a classless society. The state would cease to be useful and would wither away. Relations between the sexes would become a "purely private matter" with no need for state intervention, there would be no borders or nations and religions would disappear as they would no longer serve a purpose.

Today, revolutionary followers of Marx and Engels often call themselves socialist — particularly as the word "communist" has become associated with Stalinism in the 20th century. But at this point, Marx and Engels called themselves communists and differentiated themselves from their socialist contemporaries. In *Principles of Communism*, Engels distinguishes between different types of socialist: reactionary socialists, who wanted to return to a society dominated by feudalism; bourgeois socialists, often appalled at the worst excesses of capitalist society but who only wanted to reform it; and democratic socialists. The main concern of bourgeois socialists was to defend existing society, therefore they would resist revolutionary change. But the democratic socialists were open to the idea of system change. They were people that communists could work alongside in order to bring about a more democratic society. However, they tended to see the transitional demands mentioned by Engels as sufficient in themselves to end the misery of capitalist society and would need to be convinced in practice of the need for proletarian revolution.

Marx and Engels open their *Manifesto* with the famous words, "a spectre is haunting Europe". These words would prove prophetic. In 1847 an economic crisis led to bread riots and by March 1848 revolution was spreading across the continent. Barricades were erected in Paris. King Louis-Philippe abdicated and escaped to Britain and a National Constituent Assembly was established. The liberal assembly member Alexis de Tocqueville remarked that they had all been sleeping on a volcano.

In Hungary, nationalists led by Lajos Kossuth led a war for independence from the Habsburg dynasty and established a democratic parliament. This inspired a revolt in Vienna that overthrew Austria's conservative Prince Klemens von Metternich. According to historian Eric Hobsbawm, across an area of Europe now occupied by all or part of ten states, no government was left standing.

By May, French radicals were attempting to overthrow the assembly and in June bitter infighting broke out between radical workers and bourgeois liberals. Radicals had followed the liberals in overthrowing the monarchy, but a gulf would open up between the interests of the bourgeois liberals and radical workers. Whereas some demanded freedom of the press, others were more immediately concerned with the desperate need to put food on the table. Unlike in previous revolutions, the working class now comprised a significant force with their own demands that often went beyond those of the bourgeoisie and started to present a challenge to the economic system.

In what became known as the June Days, Parisian workers fought against the assembly in their tens of thousands at the barricades, but were eventually repressed by the National Guard, resulting in around 3,000 deaths. As Engels said: "the bourgeoisie showed to what insane cruelties of revenge it will be goaded the moment the proletariat dares to take its stand against them as a separate class" (Intro to Karl Marx, *The Civil War in France*). Marx and Engels learnt from this experience that workers could not rely on liberal forces. They would need to recognise their own distinct class interests and form independent organisations and, in a state of revolution, their own workers' governments. They began to refer to the need for a permanent revolution, which would continue until it brought about workers' power.

Across the continent, revolutionary forces were crushed by counter-revolution. Parliaments in Berlin, Prague and Vienna were shut down. In December 1848 Louis Napoleon (the nephew of Napoleon Bonaparte) was elected president of the French republic, fulfilling the hopes of conservatives for a return to order. Marx said — using wording borrowed from one of Engels' letters — that rule by another Napoleon showed that all the great figures of history appear twice: "the first time as tragedy, the second time as farce" (Karl Marx, *The Eighteenth Brumaire of Louis Napoleon*). Marx felt that the 1848 revolution failed to live up to the events of 1789. But new fronts would open up, including in Rome, where the Pope fled and a republic was declared.

Engels was a witness and participant in many of these events. In late 1847 he had attended and reported on anti-government banquets in Paris — these were a way of evading a ban on political meetings.

In early 1848 Engels and Marx were back in the Rhineland. In May, a new moderate parliament had been established in Frankfurt on the back of revolutions in many of the German states. But it was under pressure from both the workers and the aristocracy. The parliament's leaders faced the threat of counter-revolution but were extremely anxious about allowing reforms to spill over into the kind of workers' uprising seen in France.

In June, Marx and Engels set up a daily newspaper, the *Neue Rheinische Zeitung*, which called for a unified and democratic Germany. Although they were critical of the bourgeois democrats at this point their strategy involved intervening in a movement for democracy alongside the bourgeoisie, while using the newspaper to try to pull the movement in a more proletarian direction. When a Committee of Public Safety was set up in Cologne in order to defend the revolution, both Marx and Engels were elected as members. In September 1848, he addressed an audience of 8,000 at a huge outdoor meeting.

The Communist Manifesto did not have a particular influence on the 1848 revolutions; at the time it was only distributed among the Communist League's few hundred members. But Marx and Engels produced a one-page document, "The Demands of the Communist Party in Germany" that was widely distributed. However, the committee was soon shut down and public meetings banned. Engels was forced to flee to France to escape arrest for high treason. He then spent several months walking in rural France and Switzerland, sampling the region's wine and lazing about in the fields with the local women. But in early 1849 he was able to return to the struggle in the Rhineland.

Responsible for manning a barricade in the town of Elberfeld, Engels flew a red flag — made from the mayor's curtains! — before being ordered to take it down by the rest of the committee. By this time, it seemed the German uprising was coming to an end. But Engels took part in one last armed struggle as part of a volunteer company of workers and students. The 28-year-old Engels was an accomplished soldier who took part in four battles against Prussian troops. His involvement in armed fighting gave him an authenticity that would prove useful. Where other intellectuals talked about revolution, Engels had actually fought to defend one. But the campaign was ultimately doomed. After being forced to flee over the Swiss border, Engels followed Marx's advice and headed for Britain.

★ 5:
EXILE IN MANCHESTER

In 1850 Engels returned to Manchester to work for Ermen and Engels, initially taking up the same modestly paid clerk job he had done as a teenager. This suited his father. Having a son in Manchester meant he could keep an eye on the activities in Britain of his business partner Godfrey Ermen.

Engels was eventually able to work his way up the factory hierarchy, becoming a wealthy man, earning a yearly salary of over £1,000 and shares in the business, the equivalent of around £100,000 today (Hunt, *The Frock-Coated Communist*, p193). His lifestyle in Manchester became in some ways typical of a well-to-do Victorian gentleman. He was a keen fox hunter, joining the Cheshire Hunt. But at the same time as keeping an official home where he could entertain bourgeois guests, he had an unofficial address where he lived with Mary and her sister. As an exile from the Prussian state, he was also often under suspicion from the authorities.

It was a contradictory existence, advocating for workers' insurrection while at the same time managing a cotton mill and profiting from their exploitation. Part of the reason Engels reluctantly agreed to take the job was to finance Marx's career. Living with his family in Soho, Marx was spending much of his time in the reading room of the British Museum where he had returned to his economic studies. The Marx family lived in dire poverty, especially in their early years in London. Of six children in total, only three, Jenny, Laura and Eleanor, survived to adulthood. Marx constantly requested money and over the 20 years Engels worked in Manchester he funnelled up to half of his income to the Marx family.

When Marx's housekeeper Helene Demuth gave birth to a son in 1851, Engels claimed to be the father and even gave the boy his Christian name. But it is widely believed that Freddy Demuth was actually Marx's son and that Engels stepped in to protect Marx's reputation.

Marx even tactlessly wrote to Engels for money while Engels was mourning the loss of Mary, who died in 1863 (she would have been around 40 years old). This outraged Engels but, after Marx apologised, they were able to resume their friendship. After Mary's death, Engels started a relationship with her sister Lizzie, a practice that was fairly common in Victorian times. Marx's wife Jenny had disapproved of Engels' relationship with Mary, but the Marx family had a much warmer relationship with Lizzie — they had learnt their lesson about how important the Burns sisters were to Engels.

The 1850s were a time of relative passivity among the working class in Britain and in Europe. Chartism in Britain had been systematically broken. In 1857 there was a global economic crisis, which Engels hoped would lead to revolution, but his prediction was wrong in this case.

Marx and Engels had few friends among the dispersed group of German émigrés. The Communist League was disbanded in 1852 after many of its leading members were arrested and put on trial. One of their few allies was Ferdinand Lassalle, a former Hegelian and a talented and intelligent organiser based in Berlin. But they differed over Lassalle's tactics which involved trying to win over the aristocracy to bestow universal suffrage from above. Lassalle aimed at reforming the existing state — turning it into a people's state. He was also secretly involved in trying to form an alliance with the conservative German prince Otto von Bismarck against the bourgeoisie. By contrast, Engels argued that the best chance of creating the conditions for a proletarian socialist revolution in the German speaking states was the overthrow of the old feudal regime by the bourgeoisie. Lassalle died in 1864 — he was shot in the stomach in a duel with a love rival — but his ideas of state-led socialism remained influential.

In Manchester, Engels found time to continue his writing in the evenings. When Marx secured some journalistic work for the *New York Daily Tribune*, there were demands for Engels to ghostwrite the articles as his English was much better than Marx's. Engels was particularly interested in military strategy and on issues of international politics he has been described as "one of the most original thinkers in the latter half of the 19th century" (Gustav Mayer, *Friedrich Engels: A Biography*, Chapman & Hall, 1936, p142). Aided by his own first-hand military experience, he was able to write very knowledgeable accounts of the Crimean War, the unification of Italy under Garibaldi, and the looming war between France and Prussia.

In a short book, *The Peasant War in Germany*, Engels turned his attention to the militant peasant uprisings across Germany in the 16th century. His aim was to highlight the striking parallel between the events of 1525 and the revolutions of 1848-9.

In the 16th century, society was changing as industry started to grow and a middle class started to develop. There was also a huge mass of peasants who were brutally exploited. They worked on their master's estates and were forced to pay additional taxes on the produce of their own land. Communal land such as woods and meadows had been taken by the masters and sedition could be punished by torture on the rack.

The middle-class opposition to feudalism was represented by Martin Luther, who initially preached against the Catholic clergy, triggering an insurrection that drew in much wider layers of society. However, when it looked like the revolt might represent a fundamental challenge to economic oppression, Luther distanced himself from the peasant forces, much as the bourgeoisie had turned on the proletariat in 1848-9. According to Engels, Luther was so wary of the threat of peasant insurrection that he ended up siding with the Pope against them, betraying even his own ideals. The peasant leader Thomas Müntzer was able to win large numbers to his cause, but his forces were poorly armed and were ultimately defeated.

Revolt against feudalism often took the form of religious heresy. Müntzer preached in sermons about bringing about a society where all is held in common and of violently destroying those "who stand in the way of God's revelation." Religion played a key role for many of those involved on all sides. However, Engels showed how these were not just battles over ideas. There was a material basis for the formation of different classes and the conflicts between them which underpinned what might have appeared to be a conflict over religion. *The Peasant War in Germany* was therefore the first systematic work of history to apply this historical materialist method.

★ 6:
THE FIRST INTERNATIONAL

With relatively little scope for direct engagement in working class politics in Britain, Marx and Engels were still able to comment on events elsewhere, particularly the American Civil War. The war was fought between the slave owning South and the more industrial northern states, led by Abraham Lincoln. Although the British ruling class tended to support the South as a supplier of cotton, there was great sympathy among workers for the struggle against slavery. In what became known as the cotton famine, when cotton was no longer shipped to Britain because of a blockade by Northern forces of Southern ports, a quarter of the inhabitants of Lancashire were made unemployed. However, trade unions and radical MPs such as John Bright nevertheless campaigned in support of Lincoln.

In 1864, representatives of workers' organisations from Britain and France came together in London to support Polish independence (Poland had been partitioned between Russia, Austria and Germany). There was clearly an international sentiment among sections of the working class. In this context, Marx and Engels involved themselves in the setting up of an organisation, the International Working Men's Association (IWMA, later known as the First International) in order to bring together workers from different countries. It was built on the recognition that workers everywhere have more interest in uniting with workers in other parts of the world than with their own ruling class. (Despite its name, the IWMA also had female members and leaders).

Marx was soon elected to the General Council of the IWMA as one of its German representatives and would go on to become the organisation's key theoretician and activist. It was to be an organisation made up of and led by workers. The preamble to its provisional rules, written by Marx, stated that: "The emancipation of the working classes must be conquered by the working classes themselves". Marx and Engels had learnt from the experience of 1848 that workers could not rely on the bourgeoisie to win liberation on their behalf.

Involving 25,000 British trade unionists, the IWMA was behind some big workers' demonstrations for suffrage in London. It successfully organised for British workers to support a strike of bronze workers in Paris and arranged legal support for arrested miners in Belgium. The organisation laid down the roots of socialist parties in Germany, France and Italy, which would go on to form the basis of mass socialist parties.

Engels' attitude to different races ought to be mentioned here. Unfortunately, his writings on the 1848 revolutions expressed views that we would call racist today. He praised Kossuth's Hungarian uprising which was partly a nationalist movement based on Magyar culture, language and identity and in opposition to the Slavs. Engels once referred to Slavs (apart from the Poles) as "historyless" in contrast to the Magyars and Germans who were seen as playing an active role in revolutionary transformation. Part of Engels' criticism came from the fact that Slavic people often found themselves allied with the Habsburg Empire and with Tsarist Russia and he held a lifelong antipathy towards these ageing Empires — but this doesn't excuse his views (see Lindsey German, 'Life of a Revolutionary' in *International Socialism* 65, 1994, pp20-21).

However, Engels later abandoned his earlier formulations about non-historic peoples and started to support movements of resistance to colonialism, including the cause of the Chinese, Algerian and Congolese resistance movements. He recognised that colonialism often involved the plunder of resources, enriching the same capitalists in the colonising countries who oppressed their workers. Engels condemned antisemitism and started to take an interest in Irish liberation, proposing to write a book on Ireland outlining how British colonialism had kept the nation subordinated, although this was never finished. Lizzie Burns also actively supported Irish republicanism and wore black as a sign of mourning when three members of the Irish Republican Brotherhood were executed in Manchester in 1867.

The 1860s saw another success for Marx; after years of prodding from Engels, he finally finished the first volume of *Capital*. The book is rightly seen as Marx's masterpiece. *Capital* analysed how the capitalist system works as a whole, rather than merely grasping one aspect of it. It explained how exploitation of workers and competition between capitalists are the central driving forces of capitalism. As a substantial work on economics it was an invaluable tool in the various disputes Marx and Engels engaged in with socialists from different traditions.

Without the financial support and encouragement of Engels it seems doubtful that Marx would have completed *Capital*. Marx himself wrote: "it has always weighed on my conscience like an Alp that you have dissipated your splendid energy and let it rust on commercial matters, principally on my account" (Quoted in John Rees, 'Engels' Marxism' in *International Socialism*, issue 65, 1994).

Engels' insider knowledge of the workings of the factory were vital to Marx in writing *Capital* and the later chapters contain accounts of the terrible conditions for workers and especially the effect of extremely long working hours that are reminiscent of Engels' *Condition of the Working Class in England*. It was Engels who initially encouraged Marx's interest in economics with his 'Outlines of a Critique of Political Economy'. *Capital* employs an understanding of labour and alienation that is found in early works such as *The German Ideology*. And Marx also benefited from Engels' efforts to publicise *Capital*. When it looked as if the leading journals were not reviewing the book, Engels even reviewed it himself in various different publications.

★ 7: ON PRIMROSE HILL

In 1869, Engels' contract with Ermen expired and he was able to leave work in the Manchester factory. Marx's daughter Eleanor wrote of how happy he was on his last day of work: "I shall never forget the triumph with which he exclaimed 'for the last time' as he put on his boots in the morning to go to his office" (quoted in German, 1994, p23). He was able to move with Lizzie to London, setting up their home at 122 Regents Park Road in Primrose Hill, just a 10 minute walk from the Marx household at 41 Maitland Park Road.

Life in London meant that Engels could play a much more active role in the International Working Men's Association and he became its corresponding secretary for the branches in Belgium, Italy, Spain, Portugal and Denmark. In practice this gave him a huge responsibility in coordinating the movement across the continent. He welcomed a wide range of leading figures in 19th century socialism to his home, including August Bebel, Eduard Bernstein and Karl Kautsky, who would go on to play key roles in the German socialist movement, the German chemist Carl Schorlemmer, Keir Hardie, the future founder of what became the Labour Party, and the textile designer and socialist activist William Morris. Engels and his associates would often stay up until two or three in the morning drinking German Pilsner or Bordeaux and discussing politics. Engels was one of the most widely educated people of his day. He could speak at least nine languages fluently and had newspapers from across Europe sent to his home every day.

Engels would become a close friend of the whole Marx family, becoming like a second father to Marx's daughters. There were picnics and days out at the seaside for "uncle Angel", "aunty" Lizzie and the Burns sisters' niece Ellen (known as "Pumps"), often at Brighton or Eastbourne on the south coast.

Returning to his writing on the living conditions of workers, Engels wrote a series of articles on the housing question. Migration into the cities had made the apparent shortage of housing a huge cause of concern. But Engels criticised the bourgeois philanthropists' solution to the housing problem, which was essentially that workers should own their own homes. He pointed out that in rural areas of Germany, where workers did indeed own their homes and often a small garden, this meant that their employers could pay them less and let them survive on some of the food that they could grow themselves. This tended to reduce wages for all workers across industry, including those who did not own property.

Rather than a return to this semi-feudal way of life, Engels argued that there is only one real solution to the housing problem: "to abolish altogether the exploitation and oppression of the working class by the ruling class." This would involve expropriating the homes of the rich and dividing them up into dwellings for workers. Engels recognised that there was not a shortage of housing as such. The problem was that the housing was under the control of a small number of people.

In 1870, war broke out between France and Prussia, resulting in a rapid victory for Prussia and the end of Louis Napoleon's rule. A new provisional government in France, led by Adolphe Thiers, attempted to surrender to the occupying Prussian forces. But Parisians resisted this, establishing the Paris Commune in March 1871 in opposition to both the Prussian invaders and the Thiers government.

The Commune showed the possibility of ordinary people democratically running society. It was run by a council of elected and recallable delegates who were paid a wage of no more than 6,000 francs. Its members made plans to take over unused factories and workshops and run them as cooperatives, and they set up organisations to educate children as well as canteens and first aid stations. Women played an active role in the Commune, including in its armed defence. But the Commune lasted just two months before it was overthrown by the French Army and brutally suppressed. Around 30,000 of the Communards were killed by rifle or bayonet.

Marx and Engels praised the class character of the movement and denounced the murders. But they were sceptical about the Commune's prospects for survival. In his introduction to Marx's account, *The Civil War in France*, Engels showed how the Commune had made several tactical errors. Without the leadership of a disciplined Marxist organisation, some within the Commune had called for a truce with the French forces. They had underestimated the willingness of the French Army to work with the Prussians to crush the Commune: "The Prussians who held the northern and eastern forts allowed the Versailles troops to advance across the land north of the city, which was forbidden ground to them under the armistice, and thus to march forward and attack on a long front, which the Parisians naturally thought covered by the armistice, and therefore held only with weak forces" (Engels, Introduction to *The Civil War in France*).

Marx and the IWMA were seen by some as a hidden hand behind the Commune. Even though in reality their supporters were a minority within it, they were denounced by governments and the press across Europe. After the fall of the Commune, several key British trade unionists resigned from the IWMA.

A further threat came about due to a dispute between Marx and Engels and the Russian anarchist Mikhail Bakunin. A participant in the 1848 revolution, Bakunin had been arrested by the Russian Tsar and had escaped from Siberia before arriving in London. He advocated the abolition of the state and total freedom for individuals. Communism, he thought, would end up concentrating power into the hands of a state that would continue to own property and exploit the population. In essence, Bakunin's theory asserted that the state was the main enemy, rather than capitalism. "Bakunin maintains... it is above all the state which must be done away with and then capitalism will go to hell of itself," as Engels put it (Letter to Cuno, 24 January, 1872). Having set up his own organisation, the International Alliance of Socialist Democracy, Bakunin joined the IWMA with his followers and tried to convert its branches to his anarchist views.

For Marx and Engels, the experience of the Commune had shown that workers could not simply "lay hold of the ready-made state machinery, and wield it for its own purposes" (*The Civil War in France*). Revolution would be impossible without workers setting up their own state, a dictatorship of the proletariat. At this time the term "dictatorship" did not have the same association with tyranny that it does today. Marx and Engels used it to refer to a particular class temporarily taking power and organising to try to defend themselves, as Parisian workers had attempted. To imagine that workers could abolish all forms of authority and establish an equitable society without organising a somewhat centralised state seemed to Marx and Engels naive at best and at worst dangerous.

They expelled Bakunin from the IWMA over his attempts to organise a secret grouping within it. But by this time, with the defeat of the Commune and without the British union leaders, the organisation had already been neutered as a political force.

★ 8:
ANTI-DÜHRING

After the Prussian victory in the war, Bismarck unified Germany and the country emerged as a major economic power. Industry expanded and the working class started to grow. Supporters of Engels' associate August Bebel and those of Lassalle combined to form the Socialist Workers' Party of Germany (SAPD). In 1875 they produced the Gotha Programme, an attempt to reach a compromise between the two factions. The party grew in support despite Bismarck's anti-socialist laws. When these laws were lifted in 1890 the party was able to enter parliament, changing its name to the SPD (Social Democratic Party of Germany).

Marx and Engels were critical of the Gotha Programme and cautious about an alliance with the Lassalleans. As Engels explained in a letter to Bebel, one problem with the programme was that its project involved attempting to win reforms by working with the existing state rather than overthrowing it by revolution. Its only social programme was to argue that the state should provide aid for workers to set up their own cooperatives. The Gotha Programme did not mention internationalism or make a clear call for solidarity between workers from different countries and neglected the role of trade unions. As Engels pointed out, unions are a key means by which workers organise and struggle against capital.

The Gotha Programme also referred to all classes other than the proletariat as "one reactionary mass." Engels wrote that this makes sense in conditions of proletarian revolution. But in non-revolutionary circumstances dismissing people from other classes as "reactionary" risked cutting the SPD off from people they might have worked with. It overlooked the fact that members of other classes can sometimes be won to revolutionary ideas.

Engels also felt the need to counter the ideas of a blind academic, Eugen Dühring, who had become particularly influential in the German movement including with its young theorist Eduard Bernstein. Dühring put forward a complete plan for how to bring about socialism. Asserting that his theory was the only correct view, he viciously attacked both Marx and Engels. But he replaced Marxism with a mechanistic interpretation of socialism. While a lot of Dühring's appeal was due to his pragmatism, he specified what a future socialist society might look like in a very prescriptive manner. His ideas contained elements of utopianism.

With lots of new and young recruits to the SPD there was in general a low level of theoretical understanding within the party. Few had read or understood Capital. This meant that eccentric figures such as Dühring were able to win an audience with the party membership. Therefore, Engels decided that there was a need to reassert the basics of Marxist philosophy and produced the book *Anti-Dühring*, also called *Herr Eugen Dühring's Revolution in Science*, in order to do so.

Sections of *Anti-Dühring* were also made into a shorter pamphlet called *Socialism: Utopian and Scientific* which doesn't specifically refer to Dühring but does take on utopian socialism in general. The pamphlet was published in four editions in Germany and translated into numerous languages and continues to be a useful introduction to

Marxism today.

Engels described the influence of the Utopian thinkers of the early 1800s, especially Comte de Saint-Simon,
Charles Fourier and Robert Owen. The Utopians were
sharp critics of authoritarianism and of the inability of
capitalism to meet human needs and potentials. They
proposed classless societies and had egalitarian views
that were often ahead of their time. For example, Fourier
argued that the level of emancipation of any society can
be measured by the level of emancipation of women.

The Utopians' strategy was to impose a more perfect
social order "upon society from without by propaganda
and, wherever it was possible, by the example of model
experiments". Owen was involved in running a cotton mill in New Lanark in Scotland with 2,500 people.
Emphasising education, he introduced infant schools for
the workers. The adults worked 10 and a half hour days,
reduced to 8 hours after 1810, as opposed to the 13- or
14-hour days of his competitors. Owen was also able to
set up several colonies in America such as New Harmony
in Indiana in order to try to implement his ideas of social
reform. Although these experiments were ultimately
short-lived, they offered real improvements in workers'
living standards. In Engels' words, Owen provided them
with "conditions worthy of human beings." But despite
his admiration, Engels still criticised Utopian socialism
as a "mish-mash" of different theories and ideas, none of
which posed a challenge to capitalism as a whole.

Engels explained why the scientific socialism of himself
and Marx differed from the Utopian approach, explaining
historical materialism and another key concept, dialectics.

Dialectics is a philosophy for people who want to

change the world. Mainstream philosophy and science start from the point of view that the world will stay the same unless something causes it to change. By contrast, dialectical thinkers insist that everything we observe is constantly changing and developing: "nothing remains what, where and as it was, but everything moves, changes, comes into being and passes away" (*Socialism, Utopian and Scientific*). Dialectics involves the recognition that all systems, including the capitalist system itself, came into existence and have the potential to be replaced by something else.

Bourgeois thought, which Engels refers to as metaphysics, also treats the world as if it can be separated out into individual units where each part can be pinned down and analysed. Dialectics sees different aspects of the world as part of an interconnected totality.

Another key aspect of dialectics is its understanding of contradiction. Capitalism is a system full of contradictions: it has produced incredible wealth, but at the same time produced great poverty by concentrating that wealth into the hands of a tiny proportion of the world's population. Change and development arise out of the contradictions that exist in the present state of things.

Marx had made use of the dialectical method in Capital. His and Engels' understanding of dialectics had its origins in Hegelian philosophy. However, Hegel's conception of the world was limited due to its idealism. As Engels points out, Hegel held a contradictory view. Dialectics involves an open process of evolution that can go in any direction; but Hegel asserted that evolution is driven towards a particular end point by the development of what he called "the Absolute Idea." In order to move on from this contradiction, there was a need to turn Hegelianism into a materialist philosophy.

Engels' scientific socialism, based on historical materialism and dialectics, differs from Utopianism and from Dühring's approach. The Utopians assumed that socialism could be built by a small group of people setting up model societies and that these would spread throughout the world by example. But, for Marx and Engels, socialism would have to start from the conditions of existing society. Their socialism sought to explain how capitalism had arisen historically and how it could be overthrown. A new society would arise out of the contradictions of capitalism, above all through the actions of the working class.

★ 9: SCIENCE AND NATURE

In 1873, Engels wrote to Marx to explain that while lying in bed one morning he had come to the conclusion that the natural sciences were really all about matter in motion. Over the next ten years he worked on a book called *Dialectics of Nature* that would attempt to apply a dialectical understanding to questions of science and nature.

Engels' interest in science must be understood in the context of 19th century developments in natural science itself. The geologist Charles Lyell had shown how Earth's surface had undergone continuous changes, with strata being destroyed and created in an ongoing process. Charles Darwin demonstrated how species of living things are not fixed entities but are able to evolve and even give rise to entirely new species over time. Scientists themselves we coming to see change and dynamism as central to their understanding of the natural world.

Engels kept himself informed of these developments by attending public lectures in Manchester and speaking to scientific friends such as Schorlemmer. Both Marx and Engels read Darwin's *On the Origin of Species* and praised Darwin as a dialectical thinker, who dealt a heavy blow to metaphysical thinking (*Socialism, Utopian and Scientific*). Darwin was no Marxist. He was a liberal from a family of factory owners. Despite its radical implications,

Darwinism can also be interpreted in a way that stresses individualism and competition. However, this didn't stop Marx and Engels from taking his ideas seriously.

In *Dialectics of Nature*, Engels proposed three "laws" of dialectics: the law of the interpenetration of opposites, the transformation of quantity into quality and the negation of the negation. These have often been demonstrated by examples from nature. Water undergoes a quantitative change when it is heated. But this becomes qualitative when it reaches boiling point and turns to steam, with qualitatively different properties than liquid water. Consider also the way oak trees grow from acorns. The acorn contains within itself the potential to become an oak tree. Oak trees are said to "negate" the acorns from which they germinate and are then negated themselves when they produce new acorns. These "laws" can be useful in demonstrating the type of philosophy dialectics is. But if they are taken too literally, they can end in an attempt to look for rules in nature, which is more complex than trivial examples about boiling water and acorns can capture.

However, one aspect of the *Dialectics of Nature* that stands out as truly insightful is Engels' essay 'The Part played by Labour in the Transition from Ape to Man.' Here he reasserted one of the central premises of historical materialism, that our ability to labour is what makes us human. But he also argued that labour facilitated humans' evolution from our ancestors. He supposed that humans learnt to walk upright and that this then left their hands free to develop tools. The use of tools meant that they developed large brains. Engels puts the sequence of events in the opposite order to Darwin, who thought that the brain developed first and that this led to tool use. Engels' formulation is materialist whereas Darwin's is idealist, in that it asserts that brain power leads to dexterity. Archaeological evidence has since proven Engels correct on this point.

As humans and other animals act on the world and change it, the world also acts on us and drives our evolution so we are both objects and subjects of evolution. But, unlike the changes made by other species, humans modify our immediate environment in a purposeful way. However, Engels concludes that humans do not have control over nature: "We by no means rule over nature like a conqueror over a foreign people."

Sadly, Engels had to set aside his work on dialectics of nature. Engels arrived at Marx's house one day in 1883 to find everyone in mourning. Karl Marx had died not long after the loss of his beloved wife Jenny and his daughter Jenny Longuet. At Marx's funeral, Engels spoke at the graveside, saying that "On the 14th of March, at a quarter to three in the afternoon, the greatest living thinker ceased to think". In his eulogy, Engels turned again to Darwin: "Just as Darwin discovered the law of development or organic nature, so Marx discovered the law of development of human history." He concluded the speech by remarking that Marx "was before all else a revolutionist", his main goal was always to overthrow capitalist society and he had inspired millions with his journalism and, above all, his activity as a leader of the international workers' movement.

★ 10: WOMEN AND THE FAMILY

In his later years, Marx had made extensive notes on the book *Ancient Society* by Lewis Henry Morgan, an American lawyer and anthropologist who researched the native Iroquois of New York State. One of Engels' first projects after his friend's death was to produce a book based on these notes, *The Origin of the Family, Private Property and the State* (1884). Engels rushed to publish the book in order to counter the influence of August Bebel's book *Women and Socialism*, which argued that women had always been oppressed.

By the time Morgan studied the Iroquois in the 19th century, they had become monogamous. But Morgan proposed that in early human history there was a stage when "unrestricted sexual freedom prevailed within the tribe" (quoted by Engels in *The Origin of the Family*) and men and women were free to choose their sexual partners. According to Morgan, one of the earliest forms of polygamy was the consanguine family where everyone from the same generation was considered married to each other and allowed to start sexual relationships. The form of the family went through further changes and group marriage was replaced by pairing marriage, although men and women were still equal in status. His conclusions about early human promiscuity were shocking to a prudish 19th century audience.

Engels drew on Morgan's work to develop an account

of how women's oppression came about. He noted that for most of the history of anatomically modern humans, which goes back 130,000 years, we have not lived in societies divided by class. Early humans were nomadic, moving from place to place in order to find new sources of food. They built simple dwellings and had few possessions as they would not have been able to carry them. Birth rates were low and women spaced out childbirth as they could not care for more than one young child at a time.

We know from accounts from missionaries that women in these types of societies played a role in decision-making. Children and older people were looked after collectively by the group rather than being the responsibility of close relatives. Although there were some differences between the types of roles that men and women played, there was no reason why one sex should have had a higher status. Engels termed these societies "primitive communism."

Engels was limited by the amount of information on early societies available to him and some of his views have been challenged by more recent evidence. But recent anthropological work has backed up many of his claims. For example, a study of hunter-gatherer societies in 2015 concluded that pre-class societies were characterised by egalitarianism including between genders (see Judith Orr, *Marxism and Women's Liberation*, Bookmarks, 2015, p42).

Beginning around 11,000 years ago people increasingly shifted towards living in settled societies and started to practise agriculture by domesticating animals and plants. Sometimes called the Neolithic Revolution, this happened for different reasons in different parts of the world. In Mesopotamia (modern day Iraq), a series of climatic changes made it possible to settle and to produce more food and the population grew. Making use of a historical materialist method, Engels showed how, when humans changed the world around them, this also changed their own societies.

Farming involved more work than hunting and gathering, but it made possible the production of more food than was immediately needed. The birth rate went up as more people were needed to do agricultural work. Over time, a layer of people came to have more than others. Harman suggests that the land would have been divided into plots and certain families who produced more food would gain prestige as others would look to them for favours in times of scarcity. Such families faced contradictory pressures as their need to produce for themselves could sometimes come into conflict with their obligation to help other families and ensure the reproduction of the group as a whole (Chris Harman, 'Engels and the Origins of Human Society' in *International Socialism*, 65, 1994). Producing surplus food eventually meant that people could take on roles other than procuring food, including becoming leaders or soldiers. These formed the germ of what would later become class societies and eventually developed states.

Engels argued that the shift to settled societies had two key impacts on the status of women. As agriculture became more sophisticated, using ploughs and equipment pulled by animals, it became more difficult for women to be directly involved in food production while pregnant or caring for small children. And given the need for higher populations to sustain agricultural labour, women spent an increasing amount of their time either pregnant or nursing. For the first time in history, women's ability to have children became a burden which excluded them from important areas of production.

Women were tied to the home, where the reproduction of the next generation became the private responsibility of the family. They became more reliant on men.

Secondly, as some men started to gather possessions, it was important for men to know who their biological children were so they could pass on their wealth. Therefore, women's sexuality became much more tightly controlled. Engels called these changes "the world-historic defeat of the female sex." In some later types of societies, women who diverged from the monogamous ideal were subjected to extreme punishments such as having their teeth crushed in ancient Mesopotamia. Over time, these harsh punishments were relaxed, but women continued to play a subordinate role. The nuclear family eventually became the norm.

As its title makes clear, *The Origin of the Family, Private Property and the State* links women's oppression to the development of societies divided by class and the rise of ruling classes made up of "great men" who would oversee the work of others. So these divisions also took place to the detriment of most men, who despite being told they were masters of their household, were not in control of production. For Engels men of the toiling classes have no material interest in upholding the systems of oppression that come with the division of society into classes.

Engels also looks to a future society. Reflecting on what sexual relations might look like, he remarks that we will know when there is "a generation of women who have never known what it is to give themselves to a man from any other considerations than real love."

Engels' work was influential for thinkers associated

with the women's movements of the 20th century such as the anthropologist Eleanor Burke Leacock. Writing in 1971, Burke Leacock explained how Engels' theoretical understanding helped her to link demands for women's liberation with questions of social class in a women's movement that was sometimes dominated by middle class women.

But Engels' book has also been controversial. Marxist-feminist thinker Lise Vogel rightly tried to create a unitary theory of class exploitation and women's oppression rather than seeing them as two separate issues. But she accused Engels himself of this kind of dualistic thinking because at times he distinguished between the sphere of production where material goods are made and the sphere of reproduction where children are born and raised. But this is in contrast with Engels' actual aim, which was to show the complex relationship between the ways in which things are produced and how people relate to each other (see Lise Vogel, *Marxism and the Oppression of Women*, 1983, and Nicola Ginsburgh's review in *International Socialism*, 144, 2014).

Heather Brown, a more recent critic of Engels, provides ample evidence of Marx's interest in women's liberation in her 2013 book *Marx on Gender and the Family*, but distinguishes between Marx and Engels on this issue. Brown argues that Engels over-emphasised the role of technological change and saw it as determining the nature of the family, whereas for Marx there were contradictory processes within the family itself. She points out that oppression affects bourgeois women so cannot be entirely explained by class, and further argues that there were important gender divisions in hunter-gatherer societies that Marx recognised but that

Engels overlooked. The ideas associated with women's oppression, such as women being more gentle than men or belonging in the home, do indeed affect women from all class backgrounds. But it is important nevertheless to recognise that they have their roots in the rise of societies divided by class.

Engels does not have much to say about either same-sex relationships or variations in gender identity other than male or female. However, we now know that both have been common at various points throughout history. For example, indigenous North Americans recognise various gender identities, including the existence of so-called "two-spirit people." Nevertheless, Engels' general understanding of the way in which the model of the heterosexual nuclear family came about and why it endures can help understand the roots of LGBT+ oppression.

The Origin of the Family, Private Property and the State is essential reading for anyone wanting to understand women's oppression. Some feminists have argued, like Bebel, that men have always oppressed women throughout history. Others blame sexist ideas held by men, or perhaps different cultural and religious attitudes. Engels strongly refutes these views. He shows how women's oppression came about at a particular point in history due to the needs of class society. Exploitation and oppression flow from the same historical processes and the fight for women's liberation remains inseparable from class struggle. These ideas have been used by generations of socialists to argue for movements that can overthrow class society and bring real liberation.

★ 11:
AFTER MARX

As well as working on anthropology, Engels prepared volumes two and three of *Capital* for publication. Volume one discusses the production of capital by the exploitation of workers. The other volumes provide insights into how capital circulates in the economy — in other words what happens to commodities after they have been produced and the capitalist tries to sell them — and why the system is prone to economic crashes. Editing these volumes was Engels' main focus after Marx's death. It was an arduous task as the drafts Marx had left were far from complete and his handwriting was atrocious.

Engels chose to stay in Britain rather than move to Germany after Marx's death which meant he took part in the socialist movement independently of Marx. Engels had at times been pessimistic about the prospects for the workers' movement in Britain. There were trade unions but these were often dominated by skilled workers, excluding important groups such as the precariously employed, women and workers from migrant backgrounds. Their leaderships could be conservative and parochial. Engels recognised a need for a workers' party which could unite the economic demands of the trade union movement with political ideas.

As the end of the century neared, a range of British socialist movements emerged. Many of these had their own problems. The Fabian Society established by Beatrice and Sidney Webb was based on the middle classes and adopted a gradualist interpretation of socialism quite divorced from Marx and Engels' understanding of revolutionary change.

Henry Hyndman's Social Democratic Federation (SDF) was explicitly Marxist. But it tended to act as a propaganda organisation and did not engage in a consistent way with workers' struggles. The SDF split and a new organisation, the Socialist League, was formed without Hyndman. The League established the journal *Commonweal*, edited by William Morris, and drew some members away from the SDF. But this did not resolve all the problems of its predecessor organisation.

For Engels, the New Unionism movement showed the greatest promise. The 1888 matchwomen's strike at the Bryant and May factory in east London involved around 1,400 young women and teenage girls striking against low pay and dangerous conditions. Also in east London, the gas workers led by Will Thorne started to organise and demand an eight-hour day. The gas workers' union included both skilled and unskilled workers and was the first in Britain to allow women members. Eleanor Marx was centrally involved in these movements and helped ensure that socialist ideas were heard in them.

The various socialist groups and unions came together for an inaugural May Day march on 4 May 1890, which ended with a mammoth rally of 200,000 in Hyde Park. Engels addressed the rally standing on top of a heavy goods wagon, just one of the speakers' platforms dotted amongst the crowd. At this time he worked closely with Eleanor Marx's partner Edward Aveling. Aveling helped popularise Marx's philosophy and supported Eleanor Marx in her efforts to unionise east London workers. But he was intensely disliked by many on the left including Bernstein and Kautsky and widely seen as dishonest, untrustworthy and arrogant. He was also cruel in the way he treated Eleanor, which likely played a role in her suicide.

The ageing Engels, as well as acting as an advisor to the socialist movement, was still a formidable intellect. At the age of 74 he was still writing. For example he produced articles on the 'History of Early Christianity' and 'The Peasant Question in France and Germany' for *Die Neue Zeit*.

However, his health started to deteriorate. On 5 August 1895 Engels died at home of laryngeal cancer. Marx had been buried at Highgate Cemetery; the original tombstone replaced by a huge bust by the Communist Party in the 1950s. Engels did not suffer the same fate. As specified in his will, his ashes were scattered at sea a few miles out from Beachy Head near Eastbourne by a few of his close friends.

★ 12:
ENGELS' LEGACY

The decades after Engels' death saw some of the most significant events in world history. In February 1917 workers in Russia rose up and overthrew the Tsar. A second revolution in October brought the Bolsheviks to power. For an all too brief period before Stalin's counter-revolution, the Russian Revolution offered hope around the world that ordinary people could run society.

The Bolshevik leader Lenin drew on Engels' ideas to inform his important work *The State and Revolution*. Lenin argued that in any society the state represents the interests of whichever class is in power, even though it might appear to be neutral. He concluded that the proletariat would need to smash the existing state and create a state of their own that could run society in the interests of workers. Lenin was directly influenced by Marx and Engels, by their experience of the Paris Commune and by their debates with others on the left, including reformists and anarchists such as Bakunin.

Writing in 1918, Lenin noted that Engels had correctly predicted a world war as early as 1887. Engels wrote: "No war is any longer possible for Prussia-Germany except a world war and a world war indeed of an extent and violence hitherto undreamt of. Eight to ten millions of soldiers will massacre one another and in doing so devour the whole of Europe until they have stripped it barer than any swarm of locusts has ever done" (quoted in Lenin, 'Prophetic Words', *Pravda*, 2 July 1918).

Engels saw the arms race that had developed between the German and French states after 1870 and argued that their ever expanding investment in arms meant that any future conflict would be on an unprecedented scale. His historical materialism had allowed him to detect a trend that would work itself out many years after his death. Engels also supposed that such a war might be finished by revolution in one of the belligerent countries, perhaps Russia. But he did not simply think that war would create the conditions for revolution. He thought the more likely outcome would be a rise in chauvinism as workers slaughtered each other on the battlefields and he hoped that socialists everywhere would work to prevent such a war.

Marx and Engels' notion of permanent revolution would later be developed and extended by another Russian revolutionary, Leon Trotsky. Trotsky applied the theory to the specific conditions of Russia and the world in the 20th century. He successfully argued that the Russian Revolution could not rely on the bourgeoisie but that workers should form their own organisations to take power. He was arguing against those who thought there would be an intermediate phase of liberal democracy before socialism and that the working class should limit themselves to supporting this.

In Britain, the Independent Labour Party (ILP) came to prominence, becoming part of the Labour Party in 1906. Engels was a personal friend of its founder Keir Hardie but was not particularly involved in the ILP. This was in part because in later life he was increasingly reliant on Aveling — who had fallen out with Hardie — as a source of information on the workers' movement.

However, Engels' ideas were much more influential on

socialist movements elsewhere in Western Europe, particularly the German SPD. Engels was impressed by the SPD's size and organisation. A part of the world where even liberal ideas had once raised suspicion, now had a huge socialist party, the most powerful in the world. The SPD continued to grow in influence into the 20th century and was able to win real reforms for workers.

However, the SPD took a reformist position. They talked of revolution, but in practice tended to assume that proletarian rule would come about through a process of incremental reforms involving winning demands through parliament. The SPD, and especially Bernstein, took an economic determinist approach, assuming that as capitalism grew, more and more rights would be won by workers. They ultimately betrayed many of their followers by supporting the First World War, in effect siding with the ruling class of the German state rather than with the international working class.

Worse still, a crude interpretation of Engels' ideas was embraced by Stalin and the Soviet Union. This was a society with the same exploitation, competition and oppression that Marx described as fundamental to capitalism. The Stalinist interpretation of dialectics tried to turn it into a rigid set of laws which is contrary to the radicalism of dialectics in the first place. Engels' *Dialectics of Nature*, although never completed, came to influence soviet thinking on science and agriculture. The problems with the Soviet Union's approach to science were shown most starkly when there was a drive towards "proletarian science" from the late 1920s; scientists whose work was not deemed sufficiently dialectical were dismissed from their posts and even imprisoned.

Marx and Engels talked about the self-emancipation of the working class, ordinary people winning their own liberation. But both the reformism of the SPD and Stalinism were, in different ways, based on a vision of socialism as something that is brought about on behalf of workers by great men in positions of power.

Some commentators have argued that Engels produced a distorted version of Marxism and was therefore partly to blame for the misuses of Marxism in the 20th century. Terrell Carver reminds us that the question of differences between Marx and Engels is an important one, especially as Engels outlived Marx and did much to popularise his ideas within the workers' movement. So, much of what we think of as Marxism is heavily influenced by Engels. (Terrell Carver, *Engels: A Very Short Introduction*, Oxford University Press, 2003)

There were certainly differences in the approach Marx and Engels took to their work. They had different writing styles. Marx, with a doctorate in philosophy, was inclined to place greater emphasis on human subjectivity, whereas Engels was more influenced by the natural sciences. (see McLellan) Although they initially attempted to write collaboratively, Marx and Engels' later works were often written independently. They established a division of labour. Marx would concentrate on *Capital* and Engels would work on other projects including tackling Dühring.

But the idea that there was some more fundamental divergence between the ideas of Marx and Engels does not stand up to scrutiny. They evidently discussed each other's work regularly. When Engels moved to London, he visited Marx on an almost daily basis. So, it is hard to believe that Marx was unaware of what Engels was writing or that he really disagreed but didn't mention it. There is no reason for Marx to have refrained from comradely criticism of his friend's ideas.

Carver argues nevertheless that Engels adopted a more determinist outlook than Marx. He suggests that Engels was influenced by his scientific interests to suggest that there are certain causal "laws" of social development that are analogous to the laws of physics. Engels also apparently evoked a strict causal link between the economic base of a particular society — the way in which things are produced and the relations between people — and the superstructure — the ideas of that society including political ideology, religion, philosophy, etc. Thirdly, his attempt to extend Marx's thought to an understanding of nature supposedly led Engels to overlook the role of conscious human action, including the action of workers in bringing about change.

However, Engels opposed economic determinism in his lifetime. He argued that the creation of a working class under capitalism can lead to the potential for class struggle. But he did not say that struggle would inevitably result from economic conditions. He wrote that anyone who "twists" his and Marx's thinking into "saying that the economic element is the only determining one" was departing from anything the pair had ever actually said (In a letter to Bloch in 1890). An introduction by Engels to Marx's pamphlet *The Class Struggles in France* published after Engels' death, appeared to endorse parliamentary activity and reject revolution. But this was heavily edited by the SPD leadership, with many of the revolutionary parts cut out to make it appear that Engels had their strategy of gradual reform (McLellan, p51).

The dialectical approach to nature certainly does raise questions about the kind of philosophy Marxism is. It seems that, for Engels, Marxism is meant not just as a comment on political economy and class struggle, but as a worldview that can also be applied to aspects of the natural world not directly related to human relationships. However, Marx and Engels both saw humans as part of nature. They jointly stated in *The German Ideology* that the relationship with nature was the starting point of their analysis. So it is not feasible that Marx wanted to apply dialectics exclusively to the human sphere. We now know that Marx was, like Engels, interested in the findings of the natural sciences, especially in soil science and agriculture.

However, neither Marx nor Engels asserted simply that human history follows deterministic natural laws. In fact, both point out on numerous occasions that humans are able to act consciously in pursuit of their particular goals. Engels wrote in *The German Ideology* that "history is nothing but the activity of man pursuing his aims". Historical events are not driven by economics, as the likes of Bernstein came to assume, but are the result of the combined actions of workers themselves. Marx and Engels were materialists, and clearly the material circumstances in which people find themselves influence their actions. But, to paraphrase Marx, people make their own history, even if they make it in circumstances that are not of their choosing.

★ 13:
ENGELS TODAY

Two aspects of Engels' life stand out: his desire to learn about and understand the world and his commitment to changing it. The world changed rapidly during Engels' own lifetime, and has continued to be transformed since his death, but there is still much we can learn from his work.

Engels' book, *The Condition of the Working Class in England*, was pioneering in its descriptions of the way working people lived and died. It is still in print today, perhaps because there is so much that still resonates with workers fighting over pay, working hours, precarious employment and poor housing. Many of the issues Engels alerted us to are all the more relevant today when over half the world's population lives in cities.

His term "social murder" has rightly been used to describe the killing of 72 people in the Grenfell Tower fire of June 2017 after safety issues in the building had been neglected by the council and its management company. In the same book Engels vividly describes the effects of air and water pollution on the health of the poorest, still a major health issue in cities around the world.

Engels could not have foreseen that the human effect on the natural world would threaten the very existence of civilisation or predicted that climate change would bring millions of people onto the streets. However, he did understand that all humans relate to our environment in different ways depending on the type of society in which we live. This way of thinking has been used by ecological

Marxists, who recognise that in a capitalist system, fossil fuel companies are compelled to extract ever more oil and gas, leaving us careering towards ecological disaster.

His study of the origins of women's oppression makes clear that women and LGBT+ people have not always been oppressed. The rise of class society brought with it the subordination of women and all those who refused to conform to what was seen as the heterosexual norm.

Marxism is not an unchanging dogma but a method, a set of tools that we can use to help make sense of the world. With historical materialism and dialectics, Marx and Engels founded an approach to philosophy that is based on the idea that humans can exist in many different types of society and are capable of living in yet new ways.

Capitalism is still built on the exploitation of workers and on competition between rival capitalists. The labour of workers feeds the profits of capitalism but they also have the potential to overthrow the system. And the working class today is a more powerful force than it was in the 19th century. Now a majority of people around the world rely on wage labour at least for part of their livelihood and mass strikes are playing a role in global revolts.

Engels was actively involved in workers' movements, he argued that socialists should be organised together and was centrally involved in building international organisations. He learnt from his experiences. He welcomed comrades from different backgrounds into his home but he was willing to defend his principles, sometimes in uncompromising disputes with those he disagreed with.

Engels always maintained that another world is both possible and necessary. Today it is just as necessary to learn from his ideas and to fight for a better future.

FURTHER READING

All the works by Engels discussed in this book including the letters quoted are available for free at the Marxist Internet Archive: marxists.org

The *International Socialism* special issue on Engels (issue 65, Winter 1994) includes articles on his life, his Marxism and his writings on anthropology and science.

There are numerous biographies of Engels available. Gustav Mayer wrote the first in 1936: *Friedrich Engels: A Biography* (Chapman & Hall). Terrell Carver's *Engels: A Very Short Introduction* (Oxford University Press, 2003) is a good overview, as is David McLellan's *Engels* (Fontana Modern Masters, 1977). Carver also has a longer book called *Friedrich Engels: His Life and Thought* (Palgrave MacMillan, 1989). Tristram Hunt's *The Frock-Coated Communist* (Penguin, 2010) is well researched and readable.

Research on Engels' life in Manchester includes *Engels in Manchester: The Search for A Shadow* by Roy Whitfield (Working Class Movement Library, 1988) and the pamphlet *Frederick Engels in Manchester and 'The Condition of the Working Class in England' in 1844* by Edmund and Ruth Frow (Working Class Movement Library, 1995).

Alex Callinicos' *The Revolutionary Ideas of Karl Marx* (Bookmarks, 2019) discusses the key ideas of Marxism, Marx's life and relationship with Engels. His article 'Marx's Politics' (*International Socialism*, 158) gives an account of the political struggles both were part of.

On dialectics and science, Helena Sheehan has written a fantastic book, *Marxism and the Philosophy of Science* (Verso, 1993) and Richard Levins and Richard Lewontin have outlined how they apply this approach to their own work in *The Dialectical Biologist* (Harvard University Press, 1985).

On women and the family, Sheila McGregor's article 'Marxism and Women's Oppression Today' (*International Socialism*, 138), Chris Harman's 'Women's Liberation and Revolutionary Socialism' (*International Socialism*, 23) and Judith Orr's *Marxism and Women's Liberation* (Bookmarks) are all good starting points.